Peter Dixon's
Grand Prix of Poetry

Peter Dixon's main interests are being helpful
about the house, going bird watching and hoping
Arsenal lose each week. When he is not
hoovering, he paints pictures and writes poems
and stories. He writes on paper with lead pencils.
He has long arms and shortish but strong legs.
He likes Greenpeace, looking at modern art and
scallops.

David Thomas is a sixth form college art teacher
who lives and works in Winchester. In between
his teaching commitments he illustrates books
and designs games. He would never go bird
watching.

D0766025

Also by Macmillan

SANDWICH POETS:

AN ODD KETTLE OF FISH
John Rice, Pie Corbett, Brian Moses

THE LOST PROPERTY BOX
Matt Simpson, Wes Magee, Peter Dixon

ELEPHANT DREAMS
Paul Cookson, David Harmer, Ian McMillan

Peter Dixon's
Grand Prix of Poetry

Illustrated by

David Thomas

MACMILLAN CHILDREN'S BOOKS

First published 1999 by Macmillan Children's Books
This edition produced 2001 by
The Book People Ltd,
Hall Wood Avenue,
Haydock, St Helens WA11 9UL

ISBN 0 330 35544 9

Copyright © Peter Dixon 1999
Illustrations copyright © David Thomas 1999

3 5 7 9 8 6 4

A CIP catalogue record for this book is available from the British Library.

Printed by Mackays of Chatham plc, Chatham, Kent.

Contents

Ferrari Super Zimmer

You should see my grandma's zimmer
you should see my grandma's frame
silver trim – and scarlet . . .
'FERRARI' is its name.

Ferrari super zimmer
supercharged elite
    a formula ten thousand
        that whizzes down the street.

She's always first round Tesco's
roaring round the aisle
skidding past the pasta
 . . .
chicaning through the door.

The police cars cannot catch her
    she left a Porsche for dead
 . . .   then tried to pull a wheelie
and landed on her head.

Well . . .
now, the Ferrari's in the dustbin
a scarlet shattered frame
alloyed legs lie broken
    in sun
    and wind
    and rain.

Grandma lives in dreamland,
her cat and cup of tea
dreaming . . .
with her cushions
of her very first

GRAND PRIX.

My Daddy Dances Tapstep

Roger's Daddy's clever
Daisy's flies a plane
Michael's does computers
And has a house in Spain.
Lucy's goes to London
He stays there every week . . .
    But my Daddy has an earring
        and lovely dancing feet.

He hasn't got a briefcase
He hasn't got a phone
He hasn't got a mortgage
And we haven't got a home.
He hasn't got a fax machine
We haven't got a car
    But he can dance and fiddle
        And my Daddy is
           A Star.

Sammy Spook

(The curse of teachers)

Sammy was a teacher spook
and he spooked around in schools
spooking out for teachers
as they sat at desks –
              on stools.

He'd wriggle up their trouser legs
he'd make them jump and squeal
and turn them into funny things
like mud and orange peel.

He'd turn them into awful things
              – cabbages and flies
bits of string and paper
              bits of chewed-up pies!

Ms Cook she was a sausage
Mrs Cummins was a clock
Miss Angel was a plughole
Miss Ryan was a sock!

He'd turn them into ANYTHING
so be careful where you tread –
       . . . that peanut could be teacher
and that apple core –
              The Head!

13

Holiday Memories

(circa 1950)

Not for us the airport, charters to the sun
Marbella or Greek Islands
Benidorm and fun . . .
Not for us paella, octopus or squid
drinks as long as 'check-ins'
pizzas big as Spain.

No, we all went to Skinningrove
deep in Yorkshire land,
Yorkshire pud and gravy
Yorkshire wind and sand,
slag heaps grey as gasworks
beaches strewn with coal
fossils touched with mica
brontosaurus old.

We played in ironstone culverts
we slalomed in the slag.
Caught fish in icy rockpools
anemone and crab –
we picnicked by lost railroads
        viaduct and mine
built castles out of rockstone
        red as autumn wine . . .
We hid in sheds of bramble
spun on rusted wheels
rims a rime of ochre
thistles, stings and squeals.

We caught the breath of mineshafts
their gape alive with fear
– attacked with hazel coppice
arrow, bow and spear.

So thank you for Minorca
where people go to play
but I remember Skinningrove
        El Skinningrove
        Olé!

Apostrophes

Apostrophes are important
Everyone knows that!
Ask an English teacher
An Eskimo or cat . . .
Ask a living author
(the dead ones cannot speak)
Then 'postrophize your writing
– Ten thousand every week.

Sprinkle them like peppercorns
– spatter all your words
A 'ord withou' apostrop'
is 'eally qui' absurd.

So forget about your dreamtimes
Don't trouble me with rhymes
Just learn to do 'postrophes
And you'll 'av a 'mashing
             'ime.

'eter 'ixon

Fish Fingers

Fish Fingers was a clever fish
        much smarter than the rest,

At picking fishes' pockets
        he really was the best.

He pinched a pound from codling
        a tenner from a crab
        a wallet from a pollack
        and a fiver from a dab.

He once unzipped a kipper
        with a haddock swimming by
And picked a pilchard's pocket
And made an oyster cry.

He stole a crown from Neptune
He pinched a mermaid's clothes
Pushed messes in her tresses
And winkles up her nose!

The coastguards got all angry
And they caught him straight away
Whilst stealing silver starfish
In a little sandy bay.

They served him with a summons
        some peas
        and mushy chips

And that's the end of Fingers, and his nasty little
        tricks.

Questions

How old are you dear Grandad
Are you a hundred years?
Do you remember pirates . . .
giants with big black beards?

Do you remember smugglers
Kegs of Frenchmen's wine?
Pirate men and galleons
with sails as white as lime?

Do you remember cannonballs
Wreckers flashing lights?
Treasures, charts and cutlasses
Customs men and fights?

Do you remember Old King Cole
Knights in days of old?
Dinosaurs and dodo birds
Princes brave and bold?

Do you remember Roman days
Vikings in their boats?
Motte and bailey castles
Drawbridges and moats?

Oh tell me, tell me
Grandad
Of things you can recall
and was my mother lovely
and was she best of all?

A Walk with Daniel

Who are they
        – dear Grandma
who follow us around,
Tall
and dark
and silent
who never make a sound?

We call them shadows, Daniel
they too walk hand in hand,
climbing on the larchlap
dancing through our land.

Shadows?
Shadows, grandma?
 . . . You are so very wise
     but tell me
     tell me
     Grandma
     Why do they wear no eyes?

Lost Garden

There's a scareghost in the car park
and I've seen him quite a lot
His head is half a cabbage
and his nose a big shallot.

He haunts in parks of diesel fume
his head towards the stars
– in a world that's made of tarmac
in a world that's built for cars.

He walks where once his garden grew
his pumpkins by the wall
lavender and larkspur
– the evening songbird's call.

He seeks the scent of roseflower
he sighs for yesteryears

With a head that's half a cabbage
and a face that's made of tears.

School Trip

Tracy can't do laces
up
Tracy doesn't care
She drags them round the classroom
She drags them everywhere
She dragged them round the London Zoo
She dragged them right through France
and all around the disco
and through the maypole dance.

No:

Tracy can't do laces
Tracy is a twit
We don't call Tracy 'Tracy'
We call Tracy
'Trip'.

Magic Cat

My mum whilst walking through the door
spilt some magic on the floor.
Blobs of this
and splots of that
but most of it upon the cat.

Our cat turned magic, straight away
and in the garden went to play
where it grew two massive wings
and flew around in fancy rings.
'Oh look!' cried Mother, pointing high,
'I didn't know our cat could fly.'
Then with a dash of Tibby's tail
she turned my mum into a snail!

So now she lives beneath a stone
and dusts around a different home.
And I'm an ant
and Dad's a mouse
and Tibby's living in our house.

Superstar

You should see our all-star goalie
The fastest in the west
Silver wheels and spinturn
She really is the best.

Not so hot at catching
Kicking's not her thing
But see her block and tackle
See her swerve and spin!

Strikers fear her rushes
Wingers fail and fall
Midfields stall and stumble
When Di is on the ball.

All players fear her action
They crash down at her feet
Di our demon goalie
Who strikers never beat.

Muuuuuuummmmmm

Can we have a kitten
Can we have a dog
Can we call her Frisky
Can we call him Bob?
I can take him out each day
I can brush his fur
I will buy the dog meat
and milk to make her purrrr
Mum!!!

Oh . . . no . . .
Well –

Can we have a donkey
or can we have a horse
a monkey or a parrot
hamster or a snake?
Can we have a guinea pig
a peahen
or a stoat,
llama or a budgie
a rabbit or a goat?

Can we have a crocodile
gibbon or an owl,
all the zoos are closing
there's lots and lots around . . .
A penguin would be really good
keep it in the bath
a hyena in the garden
          to make the milkman laugh.

No, WE DON'T WANT stick insects
and goldfish aren't much fun . . .

Oh, can we have a puppy . . .
       Mum
           Mum
               Muuuuuuummmmmmmm.

Grown-Ups

Where are your trainers and where is your coat
Where is your pen and where are your books
Where is the paper and where is the key
Where is the sugar and where is the tea
Where are your socks
Your bag and your hat?
Tidy your room!
Look after the cat!

You're hopeless
Untidy
You lose everything.

Where is your bracelet and where is your ring
Where is your ruler
Hymn book and shoes
Where is your scarf?
You lose and you lose.

You're hopeless
Untidy
You lose everything.

Careless and casual
You drop and you fling
You're destructive and thoughtless
You don't seem to care
Your coat's on the floor
Your boots on the chair

Why don't you think
Why don't you try
Learn to be helpful; like your father and I.

Mum . . . Dad . . .

Where are the woodlands, the corncrake and the
        whales
Where are all the dolphins, the tigers and dales
Where are the Indians, the buffalo herds
Fishes and forests and great flying birds

Where are the rivers
Where are the seas
Where are the marshes
And where are the trees

Where is the pure air
Acid-free showers
Where are the moorlands
The meadows and flowers?

These were your treasures
Your keepsakes of time
You've lost them
You've sold them
And they could have been mine.

My Sister's Getting Married

My sister's getting married
and it's awful news.
My sister wants a page boy
and it's me she's going to choose!
She's going to buy a satin suit
with frills and lacy stuff,
a soppy little jacket,
with soppy little cuffs.

I'm gonna be a page boy!
Please don't tell my mates!
Don't tell 'em where the church is,
Don't tell 'em wedding dates.
Oh please,
Oh please don't tell them!

I wish it wasn't true
My sister's 27
and I am 42!

Dinosaurs

You'll have heard about us dinosaurs
In lessons when at school
Splashing round in puddles
Sploshing round in pools.

     Bodies big as buses
     Heads pink thimble small
     Tails as long as lifelines
     Around your classroom walls.

We know you think we've disappeared
We know you think we've gone
And only live in pictures
Or charts with paintings on.

     We've seen your illustrations
     We've read the things you write
     Saying that we're brainless
     and only grunt or fight.

But really –

We are still around
We live on dogs and cats
Bits of bacon butty
Eels and sewer rats . . .

     So careful when you wander round
     And don't be fooled by lies
     We dinosaurs are waiting

     And you might be surprised!

Colin

Colin was a centipede
a hundred legs or more
he trotted on the carpet
and he trotted on the floor.
He trotted through the bedrooms
and he trotted through the loo
    A hundred legs
        all trotting
            the way that trotters do.
A hundred trotting trotters
trotting all around . . .
but Colin's trotting trotters
hardly made a sound.

He trotted on the landing
he trotted on a ball
and tumbled down the staircase
and landed in the hall!

Now Colin trots on crutches
a hundred plastered legs
a hundred plastered ankles
like little plastered pegs.

So –
When it's dark and spooky
and when it's late at night
and the house is very silent
and you've switched out all the lights
Then –
if you hear a tapping
    and everyone's asleep
        you'll know it's only Colin
            and his little tapping feet.

Lone Mission

On evenings, after cocoa
(blackout down and sealed)
I would build plasticine Hamburgs
on green lino
and bomb them with encyclopaedias
(dropped from ceiling level)
from my Lancaster Bomber
built
(usually)
from table, box and curtains
turret made of chairs
radio and gas masks
tray and kitchen ware.
But:
     Aircrew were my problem
     gunners mid and rear
     radio and bomber
     nav. and engineer.

Each night I flew lone missions
through flack both hot and wild
and learnt it wasn't easy
to be an only child.

Down Jericho Way

Yesterday at 4.00
    I saved a worm
    laying in the road.

Picked it up
Threw it in a garden
Number fifty-one.

It was not a fire worm
    a rare worm
a worm with a crown on its head.

It was not a glow worm
    a slow worm
    silver
    or golden
    or pied.

Just an ordinary worm
Dying itself in the sun.

Down Jericho Way.

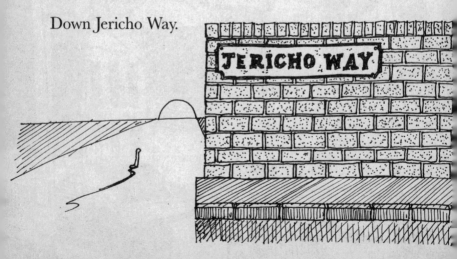

Why?

Why do cats
on winter nights
just as the goal of the year is about to be scored
appear at the window?

And why
having spilt tea
and finally
found key
and opened door
do they run away into the darkness?
Leaving me to wonder at their stupidity
and the final score.

Last Holiday

Boys and girls and laughter
Faces dancing bright
Slippers tucked in cases
Dresses daisy white
Sandals soft with beeswax
Ribbons cornflower blue
The woodland whispered welcome
But the people whispered Jew.
She left behind her suitcase
A doll
One broken shoe,
A pigtail
With a ribbon –
Faded
Auschwitz Blue.

Hot Shot Pete

Athletico Athletic
. . . big city team for me,
I'm their super striker
scoring fast and free . . .
Athletico Athletic
football silky sweet
Athletico Athletic
the best team down our street.

Visiting Winchester College

(Cloisters War Memorial – Autumn – 81)

Who are you, Aubrey Sawyerr
With two R's instead of one.
Who were you, Aubrey Sawyerr
Did you stab, and kill, and run!
Did you spring from muddied trenches?
Did you lead your men to fight?
Did you drown in shell-shocked terror
In holes of mud at night?
Who were you, Aubrey Sawyerr??
Did you whistle city girls?
Were your eyes as bright as marbles?
Was your hair a sea of curls?
Did you chase around these cloisters
Can we hear your schoolboy laugh,
Can we watch your boater spinning
And see your football scarf?
Can we read your cricket scorecard,
Can we hear you in the choir?
And see you toasting muffins
Around the prefect's fire?
Can we see you win the silver sword,
Can we see you passing out –
And see you score the winning goal
And hear the first form shout?
'Hurrah, for good old Sawyerr'
(With two RR's instead of one)
He led the school to victory
And now he's got a gun.

Oh, where are you, Aubrey Sawyerr
The farmer's soil's your home.
Eyes as black as carbon
Boots on rods of bone.
Did they kill you very quickly?
Or did you slowly die –
In fields of blood and poppies.
In fields of gas and flies?
Don't tell us, Aubrey Sawyerr,
Our day is soft and blue.
But when we walk together
Then we will talk of you.

For Brownie (the goldfish)

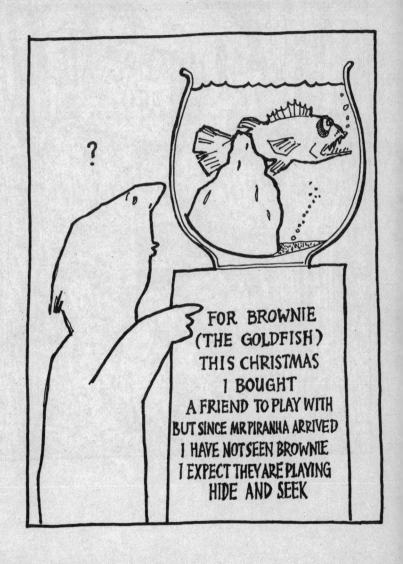

A Poem of Boxer's Lake

Boxer's Lake is dying
(does Mr Boxer know?)
The place I caught my carpfish
two score years ago.

    My world of grass and rushes
    My world of bread and paste
    setting sun in ripples
    running home – too late.
    Yes,
    Boxer's Lake is dying
    tombstone floating fish,
    white as water lily
    white as morning mist...

        White as bankside parsley
        bloated bulging eyes,
        jogging in the rushes
        jogging with the flies.

Yes,
Boxer's Lake is dying
another world is dead,
it didn't make a profit
so a price was on its head.

A Silly Thing to Do

When Father pulled a cracker
with silly Uncle Joe,
they pulled and pulled and struggled
– then Father just let go!

Poor Uncle Joe went flying,
he flew into the street
and entered into orbit
– still sitting in his seat!

You'll see him every Christmas,
he rises in the West.
Just east of Mars and Saturn
is where you'll see him best . . .

He circles earth twice monthly.
So give poor Joe a thought,
when you pull your Christmas crackers
and drink your Christmas port.

French Hedgehog

(a poem dedicated to the first hedgehog
to crawl through the Channel Tunnel)

Who battles in Kent jardin nets
Who fights le strangletwine?
Who stumbles dans les cattle grids
Who makes le chien whine?

Who picnics en the motorway
Qui eats les escargots?
Who likes a fastlane walkabout
Who rides the nightplight trail?

Who walks without a safety code
Who snorts the channel way?
Il nom est Monsieur Hérisson
    just come from France today.

Dead Cat

There's a dead cat in the roadway,
I heard the children tell.
It wears a russet collar
And it wears a silver bell.
It wears a shroud of tortoiseshell
With a pattern fine as lace
And it's lying in the gutter
With a smile upon its face.
There's a dead cat in the gutter
And it's outside number four,
Eyes as white as lilies
And blood upon its paw.
It dreams of bygone battles.
It dreams of cat-time fears,
And scratching playful children
And playful children's tears.
It dreams the stolen chicken,
The songbird slain at dawn,
And fires and feasts and fishes,
And bloodsteps on the lawn.
It smiles through ravaged thrush nests
And through the broken flowers,
And scratchings on the sofa
In the winter warmtime hours.
So, sleep your wicked catsmile,
Of secrets you can't tell.
And I'll lay you in the bushes
But, I'll keep your silver bell.

Last Waltz

Solo was a Dodo
the last one in the land.
She didn't go to parties
or dance to birdland bands.
She hadn't got a partner,
she hadn't got a friend,
until –
     she met a Panda,
     a Pandaman called Ben.

Will you dance with me? asked Solo
Can we be a party pair?
Will you take a sprig of blossom
    – will you weave it in my hair?
Will you hold me very tightly?
    – can I hold you to my breast?
    – can I snuggle really closely
       upon your hairy chest?

The woodland flutes played softly,
the evening sang its charms
    to a Panda dancing slowly
       with a Dodo
       in its arms.

A selected list of poetry books available from Macmillan

The prices shown below are correct at the time of going to press. However, Macmillan Publishers reserve the right to show new retail prices on covers which may differ from those previously advertised.

The Secret Lives of Teachers
Revealing rhymes, chosen by Brian Moses
0 330 34265 7
£3.50

'Ere We Go!
Football poems, chosen by David Orme
0 330 32986 3
£2.99

Aliens Stole My Underpants
Intergalactic poems chosen by Brian Moses
0 330 34995 3
£2.99

Revenge of the Man-Eating Gerbils
And other vile verses, chosen by David Orme
0 330 35487 6
£2.99

Teachers' Pets
Chosen by Paul Cookson
0 330 36868 0
£2.99

Parent-Free Zone
Poems about parents, chosen by Brian Moses
0 330 34554 0
£2.99

I'm Telling On You
Poems chosen by Brian Moses
0 330 36867 2
£2.99

All Macmillan titles can be ordered at your local bookshop or are available by post from:

Book Service by Post
PO Box 29, Douglas, Isle of Man IM99 1BQ

Credit cards accepted. For details:
Telephone: 01624 675137
Fax: 01624 670923
E-mail: bookshop@enterprise.net

Free postage and packing in the UK.
Overseas customers: add £1 per book (paperback) and £3 per book (hardback).